Panda

A Guide Horse for Ann

BOYDS MILLS PRESS

For our partners
in this project—Ann, Alex, and Panda.
It's been a joy to work with you.
—RH and NS

The author wishes to thank Diane Crosft of The National Braille
Press for reviewing the manuscript and offering helpful suggestions.
Grateful thanks also go to The Seeing Eye for providing information
and to Guiding Eyes for the Blind for the opportunity to help
raise guide dog puppies.

In addition, the author would like to thank Kent Brown,
Clay Winters, Larry Rosler, Alice Cummiskey, and the whole team
at Boyds Mills Press for their enthusiastic support and hard work.

AUTHOR'S NOTE
The term *blind* is used in this book instead of *visually impaired* because it is
the term preferred by Ann Edie and several of the organizations for the blind that
I contacted during the book's preparation.

Book design by R studio T, New York City
Photo research for pages 24–31 by Julie Alissi

Text copyright © 2005 by Rosanna Hansen
Photographs © 2005 by Neil Soderstrom, except where otherwise credited

Published by Boyds Mills Press, Inc.
A Highlights Company
815 Church Street
Honesdale, Pennsylvania 18431
Printed in China

Publisher Cataloging-in-Publication Data (U.S.)

Hansen, Rosanna.
Panda: a guide horse for Ann / by Rosanna Hansen ; photographs by Neil Soderstrom.
[   ] p. : col. photos. ; cm.
ISBN 1-59078-184-8
1. Animals as aids for people with disabilities. 2. Blind—Orientation and mobility. 3. Miniature horses.
I. Soderstrom, Neil. II . Title.
362.40483 22   HV1569.6.H36   2005

Visit our Web site at www.boydsmillspress.com

First edition, 2005
The text of this book is set in Adobe Garamond and Gill Sans Bold Condensed.
10 9 8 7 6 5 4 3 2 1

Panda
A Guide Horse for Ann

by Rosanna Hansen

Photographs by Neil Soderstrom
with supplemental photographs as credited

BOYDS MILLS PRESS

When people first see Panda, they usually look surprised. Sometimes they stop and stare at her. But Panda doesn't seem to mind—she just keeps doing her job.

Panda is a miniature horse. Her coat is black and white, and she has a long, thick mane and tail. Panda weighs about 120 pounds and stands 29 inches tall at the shoulder. That's shorter than most three-year-old children! Miniature horses like Panda have been specially bred to be tiny.

Panda works as a guide horse. She is one of the first horses ever trained to guide a blind person. Panda can help her blind owner, Ann Edie, go wherever Ann wants to go. When Ann says, "Panda, forward," the little horse starts walking straight ahead. Ann can't see the way, but she knows she can trust Panda. Anne's guide horse finds doors for her, crosses busy streets, and leads Ann around any obstacle in her way.

Many blind people have guide dogs to help them, but guide horses are a new idea. Ann is one of the first blind people to have a horse as her guide.

Storroton Village Museum, Eastern States Exposition, West Springfield, Mass.

When Panda is working, she wears a special leather harness. The harness has a stiff handle for Ann to hold.

Panda and her trainer,
Alexandra Kurland, meet some
young friends at the post office.

Panda is only a little bigger than most guide dogs, so she can fit into small spaces. That makes it easy for Ann and Panda to work and travel together. With little Panda at her side, Ann can ride in a car, visit a restaurant, or even take a train or plane.

Panda lives with Ann and her family in a small town near Albany, New York. "When I first got Panda, we fixed up a shed for her in the backyard," says Ann. "That's where Panda spends the night, although she often stays in the house with me during the daytime."

Ann takes good care of Panda. Every day, she cleans the stall in Panda's shed and puts down clean bedding. She also fills Panda's water bucket and feeds her. Ann grooms Panda every day, too. During grooming, she brushes Panda's coat and cleans out her hooves. This daily grooming helps Ann keep a strong bond with Panda. To Panda, Ann's grooming and care mean that Ann is her special friend.

Ann doesn't need Panda to be on duty at night, so Panda spends the night in her shed. Before bedtime, Ann gets Panda settled in her stall. "Then I give Panda some flaxseed mash and a carrot or a stalk of broccoli as a good-night treat," says Ann. "She loves broccoli! It's one of her favorite foods."

When Panda is done guiding Ann each day, she often relaxes in the backyard. She can run around the yard for exercise or nibble the fresh green grass. Other times, Panda stays inside the house with Ann. She may watch Ann preparing dinner (and hope for a broccoli snack!). Sometimes Ann and her daughter, CarolAnn, chat while Panda relaxes. Other times, Panda takes a nap on the soft carpet in the den.

Panda is housebroken. When she needs to go outside for a bathroom break, she tells Ann. How? Panda rings a bell that hangs from a ribbon on the back door. The ringing bell lets Ann know that Panda needs to go outside and relieve herself.

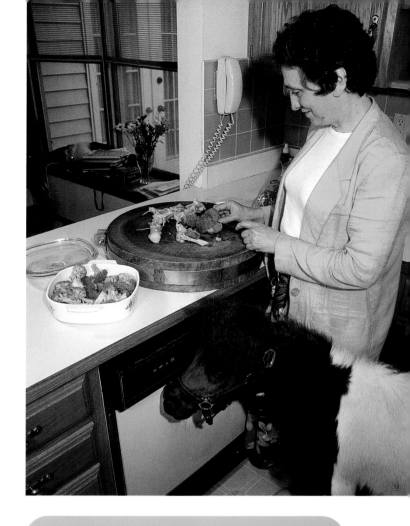

Panda Facts

Full name: Grosshill's Panda Bear

Nickname: Panda

Date of birth: January 2001

Place of birth: Grosshill Miniature Horse Farm, Ocala, Florida

Breed: miniature horse

Markings: black-and-white pinto (spotted pattern)

Height: 29 inches at the withers (the place where her back joins her neck)

Weight: about 120 pounds

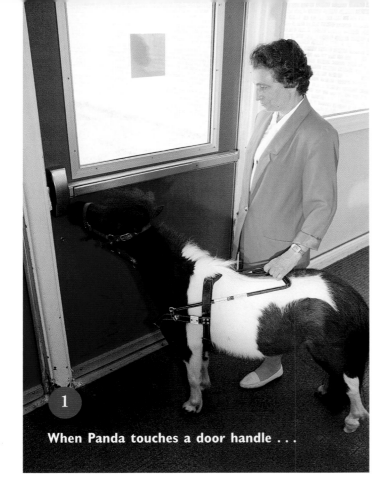
1
When Panda touches a door handle . . .

2
. . . Ann can easily locate it . . .

Ann teaches at the local high school, working with students who have special needs. Some of her students are blind, like Ann, or can see only a little. When Ann walks to school, Panda goes with her as her guide. Both Ann and Panda have the route memorized. Each time Panda reaches a curb, she stops to alert Ann. Then Ann can slide her foot forward and find the curb safely. Once Ann has located the curb, she tells Panda she's done a good job and gives her a treat.

When they reach the school building, Ann says, "Panda, find the door." At this signal, Panda touches the handle of the door with her nose. Her touch shows Ann exactly where to open the door.

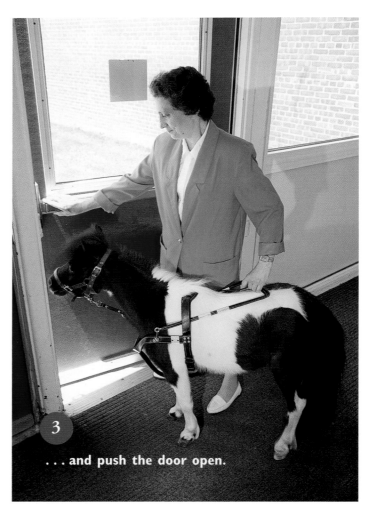
3
. . . and push the door open.

Most school days, Ann stops by her office first to check her e-mail or work on lesson plans. When they reach her office, Ann usually gives Panda a bowl of water. Guiding can be thirsty work! Then Ann may work on lessons while Panda waits for her.

Panda is tiny enough to fit in the space by Ann's worktable.

Ann has a special computer program that reads her e-mails out loud.

Then Panda and Ann head toward Ann's classroom, walking past groups of laughing, talking students. Most horses would be upset by the noise and commotion, but Panda walks calmly through the crowd. "Panda is so steady that she doesn't mind big groups of people," says Ann. "Even a hall filled with students doesn't bother her."

At first, the students were amazed when they saw Panda. They had never seen a horse in school—and such a tiny horse at that! But they quickly got to know Panda and the *clip-clop* sound of her hooves on the tile floor.

With Panda as her guide, Ann can quickly locate any room in the school. Ann knows the layout of the school by heart and tells Panda the right way to turn at the end of each hallway. Every three hours or so, Ann takes Panda outside the school to a special area where Panda can relieve herself.

Today, Ann is working on math problems with one of her blind students. For the lesson, Ann and her student use a talking calculator. These calculators are specially designed for people who are blind or can't see well. While Ann is teaching, Panda waits for her by the bookcase and takes a little snooze.

In the evenings, Ann and Panda go to a nearby stable to visit Ann's other horses. Ann grooms and rides her three full-size horses, while Panda relaxes. Panda enjoys being near the other horses, and the other horses are curious about Panda. They've never known a tiny horse before! Robin, one of the big horses, has made friends with Panda. He even lets Panda share his hay.

At the stable, Ann and Panda also visit with Panda's trainer, Alexandra Kurland (called Alex for short). Alex trained all of Ann's horses and several other horses in the stable as well.

Alex used a method called clicker training when she taught Panda. Each time Panda did something right, Alex "clicked" with a small clicker. The clicking sound helped Panda understand that she was right. Then Alex rewarded Panda with a tiny bit of grain or other food. "The clicking signal told Panda, 'You did the right thing, and you will get a treat,'" said Alex.

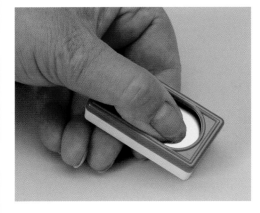

The plastic clicker that Alex and Ann use with Panda. The clicking noise it makes tells Panda that she has done the right thing.

← Alex and Panda greet two of the big horses at the stable.

Robin and Panda sharing some hay.

With clicker training, the horse always gets a reward when it does something correctly. Also, a horse is never punished if it makes a mistake. Instead, Alex helps the horse do the task again, correctly. Each time the horse does the task correctly, Alex clicks the clicker and rewards the horse.

Throughout her training, Alex gave Panda several kinds of food as rewards. "Panda loves peppermints, so I used them as a special treat. When Panda did something wonderful, she got a peppermint," says Alex. Most of the time, though, Panda's treats were small bits of grain, carrots, or broccoli.

Panda's hooves are only about two inches long and two inches wide. Here you see her little hooves next to a large horseshoe for a work horse and a medium-sized horseshoe for a riding horse.

Ann grooms Sindri,
one of her riding horses.

Besides training horses, Alex also teaches riding lessons. Ann started taking riding lessons with Alex several years ago. By now, Ann has become an expert rider. Even though she can't see, Ann can tell where she is in the riding arena by hearing the way sounds bounce off the walls. "I love to ride my big horses," says Ann. "I love the speed and the freedom that riding gives me."

Some days, Ann and Panda run errands after school. They might visit the supermarket or the pet supply store. Ann's husband, Dennis, goes with them to drive and help with the shopping. Wherever they go, Panda attracts attention. "I always get good service in a store when Panda is with me. Everyone wants to meet her!" says Ann.

In the pet supply store, Ann talks to the salesclerk about combs and brushes for grooming. Panda waits quietly for Ann and then guides her back through the crowded aisles to the checkout counter.

Waiting patiently is an important skill for a guide animal. During her training, Panda learned how to wait quietly for a long time. Sometimes she even takes short naps while she waits. (Panda can nap standing up, as horses often do.)

When Panda and Ann go shopping, people often ask Ann if they can pet the little horse. "Panda is working now," Ann explains, and asks them please not to pet her guide horse. "I like to talk to people about Panda, but it's important that they do not pet her when she's working. She needs to keep her attention on her job," says Ann.

Good Manners with Guide Animals

If you see a guide dog or guide horse with a blind person, remember not to touch the animal. Guide animals are working. They should not be petted or offered food without permission from their owners. When you pet a guide animal, it may think it's time to play. Then the animal might have a hard time getting back to work.

Some weekends, Ann takes short trips with her husband and daughter. Wherever they go, Panda goes, too. She fits easily into their van, standing right by Ann's side. Sometimes the family goes shopping. Other times they visit parks or gardens. Innisfree Garden in Millbrook, New York, is one of the gardens they like best.

Ann loves the sounds and smells at Innisfree Garden. She likes to feel interesting plants or rocks with her fingers. She also likes the *clip-clop*, *clip-clop* of Panda's little hooves on the stone paths. As Ann explores the garden with Panda, she finds gravel walks and wooden bridges—each one with a different feel under her feet.

Ann and Panda practice crossing a wooden bridge, while Alex checks their work.

Innisfree Garden, Millbrook, NY (both)

On a hot day, the mist from Innisfree's Water Sculpture feels refreshing. Ann enjoys cooling off with her daughter, CarolAnn; her husband, Dennis; and with Panda.

After their stroll, it's time for lunch. Ann takes off Panda's harness so the little horse can relax. Alex has joined them and brought a special treat—brownies for dessert. Panda's lunch is hay mixed with pellets of vitamins and minerals. Afterward, Ann gives her broccoli for dessert. Yum, yum!

When Ann puts the harness back on, Panda knows it's time to work. But Panda doesn't mind—she seems happy and ready to go. "Panda is a great worker," says Ann. "She knows we're a team, and she likes to do her job."

When Is Panda Happy?

Ann is often asked how she can tell when Panda is happy. Here's her reply:

"How do I know when Panda is happy? It depends on the situation. When I approach her house, I hear her excited little whinny. That sounds happy. When I'm grooming her and she puts her little nose up to my face and gives a soft nicker, that sounds very happy to me.

"When she's working and we're moving freely along the sidewalk at a lively trot, and she arches her back and gets an extra spring in her step, that feels happy to me. Whether we are working or just relaxing together, I can feel through her body close to mine that she is happy with her life and confident that she can do the job of being my guide very well indeed."

Innisfree Garden, Millbrook, NY

(Clockwise from left)
It's lunchtime for Ann, CarolAnn, Dennis, Alex—and Panda, too.

Guide dogs have been helping blind people in the United States since 1929. That year, a group called The Seeing Eye began training German shepherds as guide dogs. Since then, thousands of dogs have been trained by The Seeing Eye and other organizations. German shepherds, Labrador retrievers, and golden retrievers are the breeds most commonly used as guide dogs today.

Guide horses, on the other hand, are still a new idea. Cuddles, the first full-time guide horse, began work in 2001. The same year, Panda began her training. Since then, Cuddles, Panda, and a handful of other miniature horses have been showing the world that minihorses can be safe, reliable guides for the blind.

Cuddles lives and works with her blind owner, Dan Shaw, in Ellsworth, Maine. She began guiding Dan full-time in 2001. Before that, Cuddles was trained as a guide by Don and Janet Burleson of Kittrell, North Carolina.

Cuddles and Dan Shaw practicing a street crossing.

The Burlesons were the first people to think miniature horses could be guides. They got the idea from watching Twinky, one of their pet miniature (mini) horses. Twinky was friendly and patient and seemed to have natural talent as a guide. Don and Janet started wondering if minihorses could learn to guide blind people, the way that guide dogs do.

In 1999, the Burlesons started training Twinky, spending many hours teaching her to be a guide. Twinky learned quickly and soon knew basic guiding skills. The Burlesons were excited about Twinky's progress and decided to train another minihorse as a guide. This time, they hoped to place the guide horse with a blind person.

Don and Janet Burleson (above) with one of their pet minihorses. Twinky (right), the first mini trained as a guide, sometimes wears little sneakers on her hooves to protect them.

Lisa Carpenter (2)

By early 2000, Ann Edie heard that the Burlesons had trained a minihorse as a guide. Ann was intrigued by their project right away. "I felt from my own experience that horses are smart enough to do guiding work," said Ann. "But I didn't know there were minihorses the right size to be a guide until I heard about Twinky."

When she first heard of the Burlesons' work, Ann owned a wonderful guide dog named Bailey. For years, Ann and Bailey went everywhere together, and the dog had become a beloved member of Ann's family. But Bailey was already ten years old. Most guide dogs retire after seven or eight years of service, so Ann knew Bailey wouldn't be able to work much longer.

Bailey was Ann's guide dog for nine years.

Then, in October 2000, Bailey suddenly got sick and died, just four days after his eleventh birthday. Ann had lost her guide and dear friend. She was very sad and missed Bailey terribly. Ann couldn't bear the thought of getting another guide dog right away.

For a while, Ann used a long white cane to get around. Many blind people are trained to use these canes. But Ann missed the freedom a guide animal gave her. She started to think about getting another guide dog, or perhaps even trying a guide horse. Ann knew that horses lived much longer than dogs—often as long as thirty years. That meant she could have a horse as her guide for many years.

Ann shows how her white cane can be folded up for storage.

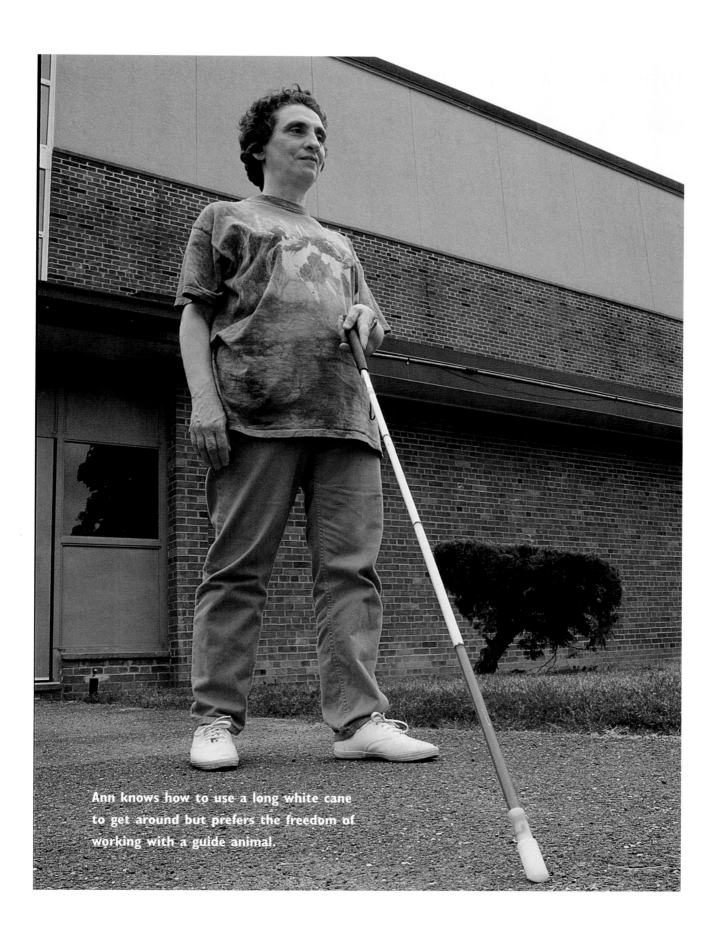

Ann knows how to use a long white cane to get around but prefers the freedom of working with a guide animal.

Todd Sumlin

During these difficult months for Ann, the Burlesons were busy teaching Cuddles to be a guide. In her advanced training, Cuddles began working with Dan Shaw. If Cuddles and Dan could learn to be a team, Cuddles would go to work as Dan's full-time guide.

When Ann heard about Cuddles and Dan, she wanted to learn more about them. Alex Kurland was intrigued, too. In May 2001, Ann and Alex flew down to North Carolina to meet Cuddles, Dan, and the Burlesons.

Ann and Alex were impressed with the way Cuddles and Dan worked together. Busy streets, stairs, overhead obstacles—Cuddles and Dan could handle them all.

A few days later, Dan and Cuddles "graduated" from their training and headed to Dan's home in Maine. They were now the first blind person and guide horse ever to work together on their own—and suddenly they were famous! Cuddles, Dan, and the Burlesons were featured in news reports around the world.

Cuddles and Dan ride a subway train with Don and Janet Burleson.

Erik Lesser

Meanwhile, Ann and Alex were excited by what they had learned. It looked as though minihorses could become fully satisfactory guides for blind people. The little horses are well suited for guide work. They see very well all around them, and have especially good side vision. They also have a calm nature and are affectionate creatures.

Sometimes Cuddles wears a special sign that tells people she's working.

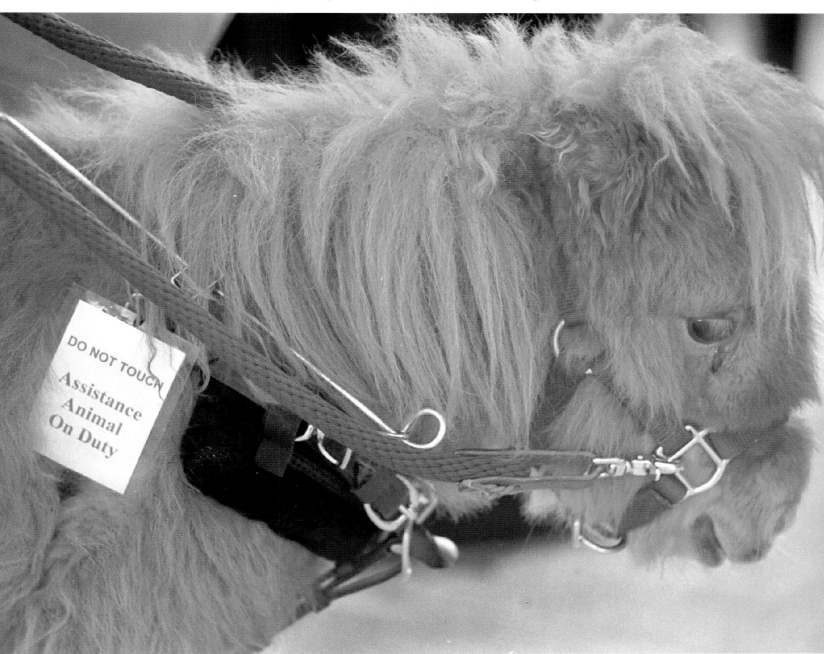

Todd Sumlin/The Charlotte Observer

After meeting Cuddles, Ann and Alex made a big decision. They decided to get a minihorse and train it themselves. Then Ann could find out firsthand what it is like to have a guide horse.

For months, Ann and Alex searched the Internet to find a listing for the right little horse. At the same time, they planned their training program. They wanted the training to be a detailed research project. That way, Ann and Alex could help answer some of the questions people still had about guide horses:

- Are most minihorses smart enough to learn guide work, or were Twinky and Cuddles unusually smart?
- Can minihorses learn to do all the tasks guide dogs do?
- Can these horses live and work in human places, like schools and houses? Can they live and work that way for a long time?

Twinky and Cuddles had already accomplished a lot and answered many questions. But they were only two horses—and might be unusual. Could more minihorses learn guide work? If more minis could be trained, it would help show that many of these horses could become guides. So, Ann and Alex started looking for the right mini to train.

Erik Lesser

Guide horses are small enough to travel on airplanes. Here, Cuddles stays close to Dan during a plane trip.

Michael C. York/AP Wide World Photos

Dan and Cuddles sometimes go for walks in Acadia National Park in Maine. The rocky hills are a big challenge, but Cuddles leads Dan with ease and confidence. As you can see, Cuddles is wearing little sneakers to protect her hooves from the rocks.

After months of searching, Ann and Alex found a nine-month-old filly (young female horse) that seemed perfect. Her name was Panda Bear (Panda for short), and she lived at Grosshill Miniature Horse Farm in Florida. Panda seemed calm and easy to handle. Also, she was tiny. At nine months old, she stood only 24 inches tall at the shoulder, or withers (where her back and neck meet).

Ann bought Panda, and the little horse arrived from Florida in September 2001. At first, Panda went to live with Alex. That way, Alex could train her every day. Alex fixed up a special stall for Panda in the garage by her house.

Before Alex could teach Panda guiding skills, Panda needed to learn how to live

with people. She had to learn to walk on a lead, go up and down stairs, and ride in a car. Most important, she needed to be housebroken.

Each day, Alex taught Panda new skills. One of the first things Panda learned was to place her front hooves on a training platform. Once Panda had mastered that, she learned to climb up the steps of Alex's house. Whenever Panda did a task correctly, Alex would click the clicker and give her a reward.

"Panda learned to climb stairs without any problem," Alex says. "Now she likes to climb up my stairs and pose proudly at the top. Sometimes I think she's a mountain goat, not a horse."

1. Panda gets ready to jump into Alex's car.

2. Success! Panda fits nicely into the back of the car. And the special plywood floor is easy for Panda to stand on.

3. Panda can put her head up between the front seats to say hello. The blanket between the seats helps keep Panda the right distance from Alex.

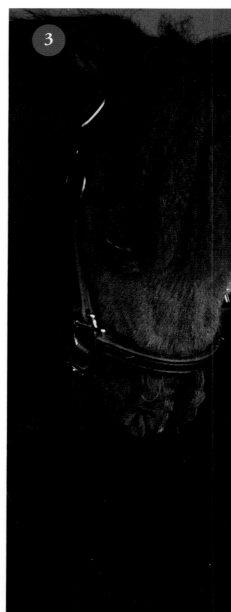

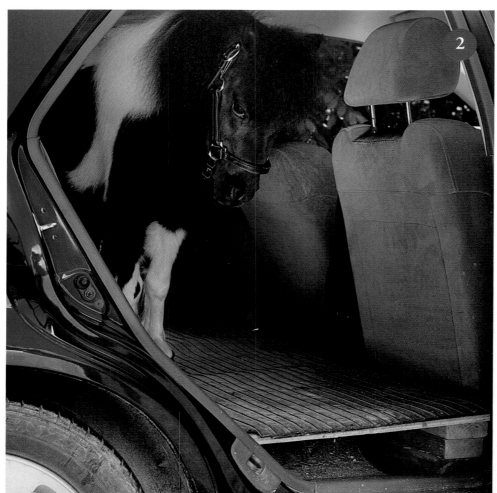

Panda also learned to ride in Alex's car. To make room, Alex removed the backseat of her car and put in a plywood floor. Panda learned to put her front hooves up on the plywood and jump inside the car. "Panda wasn't very graceful at first, but she kept trying. Now she hops up in my car or Ann's van without any trouble," Alex says. "Panda is very steady and surefooted, so she doesn't have any trouble keeping her balance as the car is moving."

If cars had seatbelts that were shaped right for horses, Panda would wear a seatbelt. But no one has invented the right kind of seatbelt for her yet. As guide horses become more common, a guide-horse seatbelt may become available. Alex and Ann hope so—they would love for Panda to have her very own seatbelt in Alex's car and Ann's van.

Early in her training, Alex took Panda on walks around the neighborhood. First, Alex would take Panda's harness and leash in her left hand. Then she'd say, "Panda, forward," while she motioned forward with her right hand. Panda quickly learned to walk straight ahead when Alex gave her these signals.

As they walked, Alex taught Panda to stay by the edge of the road and to stop at curbs. Alex also taught Panda to guide her around parked cars, trash cans, low branches, and other obstacles. Some days, Alex and Panda would practice walking to the nearby mailbox. When Alex told her, "Find the mailbox," Panda learned to walk right up and touch it with her nose. Click and treat—a peppermint for Panda!

Soon, Alex took Panda downtown for lessons. The post office was a perfect spot for Panda to practice walking up and down stairs. And all the postal workers got to meet the little horse when Alex and Panda went inside to get stamps or mail packages.

When Panda touched the mailbox with her nose, she got a treat—and then Alex could drop her letters into the box.

When Panda's lessons were done, Alex let her run free in the backyard. "Go be a horse, Panda," Alex would say as she took off Panda's harness. Panda knew that meant playtime! She could run through the yard and garden as much as she liked. "She loved to leap over flowerbeds and race around the bird feeder," said Alex. After playtime, Alex and Panda would head to the stable to visit the other horses and say hello to the barn cat, Tobie.

←At playtime, Panda loved to run through the backyard.

↑ Panda made friends with the barn cat, Tobie.

Several months later, Panda was ready to work with Ann. At first, Ann and Panda stayed in Ann's neighborhood, with Alex checking Panda's work. Soon, Panda began to train with Ann in school and on shopping trips downtown.

Every guide animal must learn how to cross a busy street safely. Alex had spent many hours working with Panda on street crossings. Now it was Ann's turn. When Ann and Panda approached the street crossing, Panda led Ann to the curb and stopped. Then Ann found the curb with her foot and listened to the traffic noise.

While Ann listened, Panda watched the traffic go by and waited for Ann's signal. (Horses can't tell if the traffic lights are red or green, so Panda is not trained to look at the lights.) When Ann heard the noise of the cars in front of her stop, she knew it was safe to cross. "Panda, forward," Ann said, and gave her horse the forward hand signal. Panda walked briskly ahead, and they crossed the street with time to spare. "Good girl, Panda!" said Ann, and gave her horse a click and a special treat.

If Panda had seen something dangerous when she watched the traffic, she would have refused to move when Ann told her to go forward. This skill is called "intelligent disobedience," and all guide animals need to learn it.

Ann and Panda waited for the traffic to stop, while Alex watched them work together.

When it was safe to go, Ann
and Panda walked briskly
across the street.

41

After training in Ann's hometown for several months, Panda was ready for a new challenge. So Ann and Alex took Panda to Albany, the capital city of New York State. There, Panda could learn about crowds, busy traffic, and lots of noise.

Albany was a big new world for Panda, but it didn't upset her. She guided Ann past tall buildings, through crowded streets, and even around construction sites. During their trip, Ann needed to visit the Albany State Library. The library had a new challenge: a long, steep set of stairs. To Panda, the stairs must have looked as high as a mountain.

"Panda, find the stairs," Ann told her. *Tap, tap.* Panda tapped her front hoof on the first step to tell Ann where it was. "Panda, forward," said Ann. Sure enough, Panda led her up and down those stairs like she'd been climbing them for years. "Good girl, Panda!" said Ann, as she gave Panda a special treat.

(top) Panda carefully led Ann around the barrier and bricks at this construction site.

(bottom) The library stairs are long and steep! But Ann and Panda took them right in stride.

Another time, Ann and Panda visited the Albany train station. There they practiced taking an elevator, walking through the busy station, and getting on a train. The train conductor was surprised to see a minihorse, but Panda seemed relaxed the whole time.

The summer of 2003, Panda went to live with Ann full time. Sometimes Alex watched their training sessions. But soon, Ann and Panda were working all on their own—and loving it! As they worked together, Ann and Panda became real partners. Each time they practiced, they gained confidence and learned to trust each other. Panda worked smoothly and easily with Ann, understanding her needs.

By September, Ann knew Panda was ready to "graduate" and become her full-time guide. When Ann went back to her teaching job, Panda went with her as her guide horse. "Panda and I had become a team, and that is a marvelous feeling!" said Ann.

That fall, Ann and Panda had many new adventures together. They took their first long car trip and then had Thanksgiving dinner with twenty of Ann's relatives. Panda was a perfect guest, despite the holiday commotion. While Ann feasted with her family, Panda dozed quietly in the front hall. Panda learned some new skills that fall, too—such as picking up Ann's keys for her if Ann dropped them.

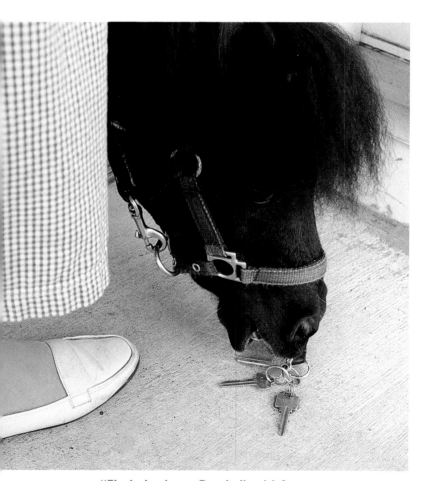

"Find the keys, Panda," said Ann.

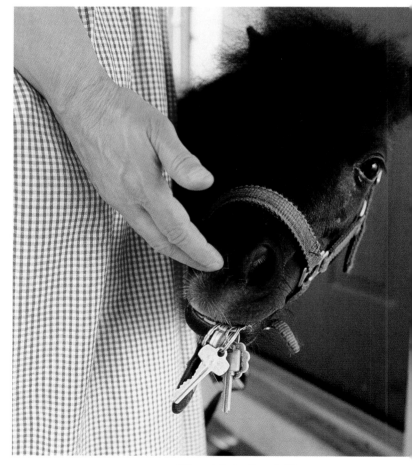

"Good job, Panda!"

After a year of guide work, Panda had answered almost all of Ann's and Alex's questions about guide horses. She had shown that horses are smart enough to learn how to guide. Panda had also shown that horses can live and work with humans. Whenever she guided Ann, Panda kept her mind on her job and always had good manners. Best of all, Panda likes her job and loves Ann.

Ann and Panda's story is still unfolding, and Panda has a few advanced guiding skills yet to learn. But Panda has already proven to Ann that she is a talented, reliable guide—and a wonderful friend. With Panda by her side, Ann can walk into the future with confidence and joy.

For More Information

Web Sites

www.theclickercenter.com
Alexandra Kurland's Web site has information on clicker training for horses and on Panda's training in particular. To read more about Panda, go to the Web site listed above, click "Enter" and then click on "Panda Project."

www.guidehorse.com
Don and Janet Burleson's Web site has information on Cuddles, Twinky, other miniature horses, and many related topics.

www.dancuddles.com
Dan Shaw's Web site tells about his guide horse, Cuddles, and their life together.

Books to Read

Cuddles the Guide Horse by Janet Burleson, RampartTechpress, 2004
A Guide Dog Puppy Grows Up by Caroline Arnold, Harcourt Brace, 1991
Guide Dogs by Judith Janda Presnall, KidHaven Press, Gale Group, 2002
Miniature Horses by Dorothy Hinshaw Patent, Dutton, 1991

Index

About the Author

Rosanna Hansen has worked in children's books as a publisher, editor-in-chief, and author. Most recently, she served as publisher and editor-in-chief of Weekly Reader, supervising the company's magazine and book publishing. Before that, she was group publisher of Reader's Digest Children's Books.

Rosanna has written over fifteen children's books on such topics as animals, nature, and astronomy. In her free time, she volunteers for Guiding Eyes for the Blind and for wildlife organizations such as the Cheetah Conservation Fund.

She and her husband, Corwith, live in Tuckahoe, New York.

About the Photographer

Neil Soderstrom is a photographer, writer, book editor, and author agent. He especially loves to photograph plants, animals, and interesting people. "What could have been more interesting," he says, "than photographing Ann Edie and Alexandra Kurland during their gentle, loving training of the remarkable little Panda?" Neil's Panda photos have appeared in *Parade, Ranger Rick*, and *Equine Journal*—and in books.

Neil lives with his wife, Hannelore, in Wingdale, New York, near their beloved Appalachian Trail in the foothills of the Berkshire Mountains.